LET'S FIND WEDGES

by Wiley Blevins

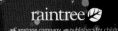 raintree
a Capstone company — publishers for children

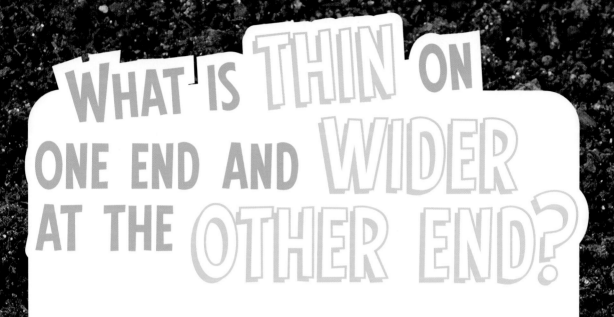

WHAT IS THIN ON ONE END AND WIDER AT THE OTHER END?

A wedge! It's a simple machine. It can cut things. Chop! It can break things apart. It can hold things in place too.

Where can you find wedges? You don't have to look too far. They are all around us!

LOOK IN THE MIRROR.

What can you see? You can see a whole set of wedges. They're smiling back at you. They're your teeth.

CHOMP! CHOMP! THEY HELP TO BREAK APART YOUR FOOD.

BRR! IT'S COLD.

A man needs wood for a fire. He grabs an axe. It is a metal wedge.

CHOP! CHOP! STACK THE LOGS.

HOW ELSE CAN YOU STAY WARM?

Zip! Zip up your coat and keep out the cold.

A ZIP USES WEDGES TO OPEN AND CLOSE.

BACK AND FORTH. BACK AND FORTH.

Have you seen this wedge at work?

A SAW IS A WEDGE THAT CUTS WOOD.

HOW CAN YOU KEEP A DOOR OPEN?

Push a wedge under it. That's all you do!

NOW THE DOOR WON'T MOVE.

A TRAIN'S POINTY NOSE IS A WEDGE.

It CUTS THROUGH THE AIR AS THE TRAIN SPEEDS DOWN THE TRACK.

WHOOSH!

The big white boat pushes through the deep blue water. A boat has a big wedge at the front.

IT'S CALLED THE BOW.

It's TIME FOR LUNCH.

Let's make a salad. A knife is a sharp wedge that cuts vegetables into small pieces.

CHOP!

HOW DO YOU CUT PAPER?

You need scissors!
Squeeze the handles.
Two wedges work
together. **CUT!**

NOW YOU HAVE PRETTY PAPER HEARTS.

TIME TO PLANT A GARDEN!

You need to dig in the soil. How? Use a spade. The bottom is a metal wedge. It breaks through the ground.

DIG SOME HOLES. THEN WATCH YOUR PLANTS GROW!

HERE IS A SPECIAL NOTE.

A pin holds it up. A pin has a sharp point. It is a wedge.

It BREAKS THROUGH PAPER TO KEEP IT ON THE BOARD.

BANG! BANG!

Hit the nail with a hammer. The nail is a wedge.

It PUSHES THROUGH THE WOOD TO HOLD TWO PIECES TOGETHER.

IN AND OUT THE NEEDLE GOES.

A needle is a wedge that pushes through fabric. Sew pieces together with a needle and thread.

WHAT WILL YOU MAKE?

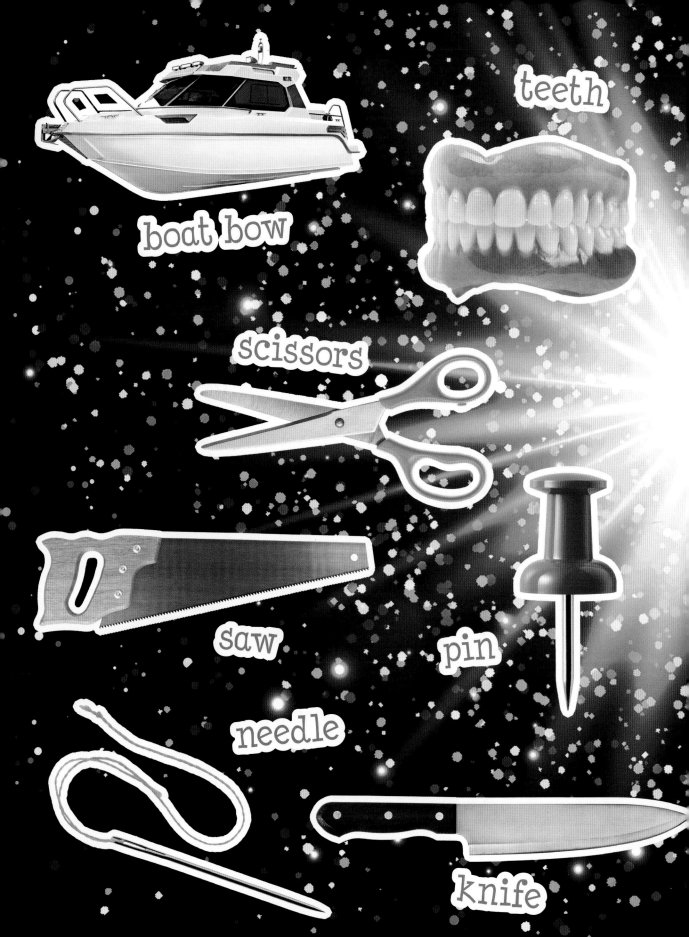

boat bow

teeth

scissors

saw

pin

needle

knife

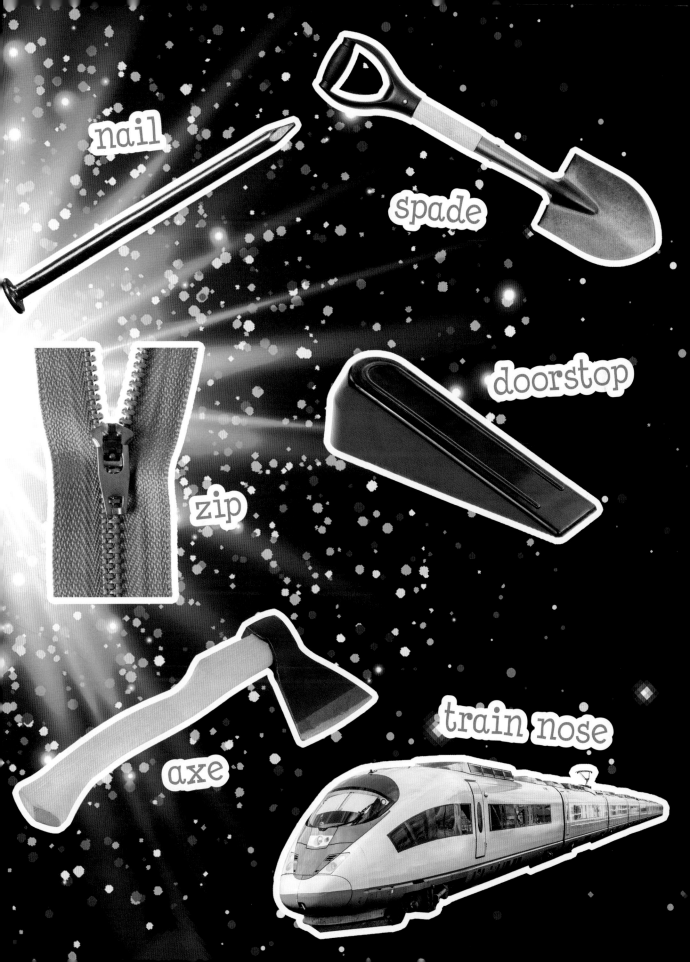

nail

spade

doorstop

zip

axe

train nose

Raintree is an imprint of Capstone Global Library Limited, a company incorporated in England and Wales having its registered office at 264 Banbury Road, Oxford, OX2 7DY – Registered company number: 6695582

www.raintree.co.uk
myorders@raintree.co.uk
Copyright © Capstone Global Library Limited 2022

ISBN 978 1 3982 0505 5 (hardback)
ISBN 978 1 3982 0506 2 (paperback)

Edited by Erika Shores
Designed by Kyle Grenz
Media Researcher: Tracy Cummins
Production by Spencer Rosio
Originated by Capstone Global Library Ltd
Printed and bound in India

Image Credits
iStockphoto: emholk, 22–23, malerapaso, 30 middle right, Marilyn Nieves, 8–9, robcruse, 12–13; Shutterstock: aapsky, 31 bottom right, Andrey Eremin, 30 middle left, Atstock Productions, 26–27, Butterfly Hunter, 30 top middle, Dragon Images, 20–21, Fast flash, 30 bottom right, Gecko Studio, 30 top right, Hurst Photo, 31 middle left, junpinzon, 24–25, KK Tan, 4–5, Kozak Sergii, Cover, Louella938, 31 middle right, Madlen, 2–3, Matveev Aleksandr, 30 top left, MrVander, Design Element, Nikita Rublev, 31 bottom left, Olivkairishka, 6–7, Ortodox, 14–15, Paul Vinten, 16–17, Phoderstock, 10–11, Shift Drive, 18–19, Tatyana Vyc, 28–29, trekandshoot, 31 top left, Vadym Zaitsev, 31 top right, You Touch Pix of EuToch, 30 bottom left

British Library Cataloguing in Publication Data
A full catalogue record for this book is available from the British Library.

FIND OUT MORE ABOUT SIMPLE MACHINES BY CHECKING OUT THE WHOLE SERIES!

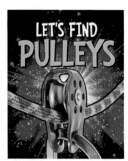